For my brother, Robert—with love (forever, of course!)
—MB

For all the artists, who live forever through their work.
—JH

Selected Bibliography

Anton, Ted. *The Longevity Seekers: Science, Business, and the Fountain of Youth*. Chicago: University of Chicago Press, 2013.

Boston University School of Medicine New England Centenarian Study; bumc.bu.edu/centenarian

Buettner, Dan. *The Blue Zones: 9 Lessons for Living Longer from the People Who've Lived the Longest*. New York: National Geographic Society, 2012.

Cave, Stephen. *Immortality: The Quest to Live Forever and How It Drives Civilization*. New York: Crown Publishers, 2011.

Critser, Greg. *Eternity Soup: Inside the Quest to End Aging*. New York: Harmony Books, 2010

Gollner, Adam Leith. *The Book of Immortality: The Science, Belief, and Magic Behind Living Forever*. New York: Scribner, 2013.

Gruman, Gerald J. *A History of Ideas about the Prolongation of Life: The Evolution of Prolongevity Hypotheses to 1800*. Philadelphia: American Philosophical Society, 1966.

Gupta, Sanjay. *Chasing Life: New Discoveries in the Search for Immortality to Help You Age Less Today*. New York: Warner Wellness, 2007.

Learn.Genetics; "Are Telomeres the Key to Aging and Cancer?"; learn.genetics.utah.edu

Olshansky, S. Jay, and Bruce A. Carnes. *The Quest for Immortality: Science at the Frontiers of Aging*. New York: Norton, 2001.

PBS Video; "Can We Live Forever?"; video.pbs.org

Stipp, David. *The Youth Pill: Scientists at the Brink of an Anti-Aging Revolution*. New York: Portfolio, 2010.

TED Talks; "Experiments That Hint at Longer Lives"; Cynthia Kenyon; ted.com/talks

University of Delaware Library, Special Collections; "Philosopher's Stone"; lib.udel.edu

Weiner, Jonathan. *Long for This World: The Strange Science of Immortality*. New York: Ecco, 2010.

Wolpert, Lewis. *You're Looking Very Well: The Surprising Nature of Getting Old*. London: Faber & Faber, 2011.

Text © 2015 Maria Birmingham
Illustrations © 2015 Josh Holinaty

Owlkids Books acknowledges the financial support of the Canada Council for the Arts, the Ontario Arts Council, the Government of Canada through the Canada Book Fund (CBF) and the Government of Ontario through the Ontario Media Development Corporation's Book Initiative for our publishing activities.

Published in Canada by
Owlkids Books Inc.
10 Lower Spadina Avenue
Toronto, ON M5V 2Z2

Published in the United States by
Owlkids Books Inc.
1700 Fourth Street
Berkeley, CA 94710

Library and Archives Canada Cataloguing in Publication

Birmingham, Maria, author
    A beginner's guide to immortality : from alchemy to avatars / written by Maria Birmingham ; illustrated by Josh Holinaty.

Includes index.
ISBN 978-1-77147-045-2 (bound)

    1. Immortalism--Juvenile literature. I. Holinaty, Josh, illustrator II. Title.

BF1999.B57 2015   j130   C2014-908458-7

Library of Congress Control Number: 2015900226

Edited by: John Crossingham and Jessica Burgess
Designed by: Alisa Baldwin

Manufactured in Dongguan, China, in March 2015, by Toppan Leefung Packaging & Printing (Dongguan) Co., Ltd.
Job #BAYDC17

A   B   C   D   E   F

Publisher of Chirp, chickaDEE and OWL
www.owlkidsbooks.com

CONTENTS

INTRODUCTION
Thanks, but I Think I'll Pass on the Whole Dying Thing

Human beings have been trying to figure out a way to live forever since...well, forever. Throughout history, we have searched for mythical potions and places that will guarantee us immortality, or eternal life on Earth.

The quest to cheat death continues even today. But rather than locking ourselves away somewhere mixing together potions, or traveling great distances in the hopes of finding a secret spring of life, many of us are turning to science and technology to extend our lives. Our focus is on using genetics, robotics, and computers to prevent death.

If the idea of living forever seems completely ridiculous to you, consider this: humans already live longer today than in centuries past thanks to advances in science, improved medicine and sanitation, and an increased supply of food and clean water.

We've managed to more than double our lifespan in the past two centuries. A person born in the early 1800s had an average life expectancy of 35 years. Today, the average life expectancy for a person in a developed country is 78 years. Maybe the idea of extending life several more decades isn't that much of a stretch. But living forever?

Many people say, Why not? They believe aging is a glitch in our lives that we should be able to fix if we try hard enough. So settle in as we learn how human beings have tried—and continue to try—to unearth the secret of how to live forever.

Find an Elixir
or Other Magical Substance

For centuries, it was commonly believed that magical substances or potions held the secret to eternal life. Ancient legends and myths told stories of special drinks and foods that bestowed immortality on those who consumed them. These tales persuaded many adventurers to set off on long expeditions in search of eternal life.

During the Middle Ages, a medieval science known as alchemy focused on potions in its search for immortality. Considered an early form of chemistry, alchemy was a combination of scientific experiments, spirituality, and "magic." Alchemists, those who practiced this approach, were determined to create the elixir of life—a potion said to grant its drinker immortality or eternal youth. Of course, there was a problem with this plan: no one knew how to successfully create this elixir. (Or if they did, they weren't saying.) Still, many tried.

This search for a remedy for death became the life's work of countless alchemists. They toiled in their laboratories from morning to night, day after day, mixing ingredients of all sorts. And this was serious business, since an unsuccessful elixir could have lethal consequences. Many alchemists died after gulping down their own concoctions.

We can all agree that "death by elixir" is a far cry from living forever. But let's give this history of potions and magical substances a closer look.

A STORY AS OLD AS TIME

The theme of immortality is seen in the folklore and legends of almost every culture throughout time. These tales show us how the desire to live forever is a thread that binds all human beings. No matter where we come from, we seem to be captivated by the idea of eternal life.

Finding Forever

One of the first stories ever written tells the tale of a man's search for immortality. *The Epic of Gilgamesh* was created in about 2000 BCE—on 12 clay tablets, no less. The hero, Gilgamesh, is told of a plant found on the seafloor that restores youth. He is so determined to find it that he ties rocks to his feet and sinks to the bottom of the sea. He finds the mysterious plant, but eternal life is not to be his. On his journey home, Gilgamesh stops to take a swim. He leaves the plant on the shore, where it's stolen by a snake. As it slithers away, the snake sheds its skin and becomes young again. And Gilgamesh learns that you should never take your eyes off the prize.

Gilgamesh was a real historical figure. He reigned as king of the Mesopotamian city of Uruk around 2700 BCE.

The Search Is On

During his reign, from 221 BCE to 210 BCE, Chinese emperor Qin Shi Huang made three visits to an island off the coast of China. He hoped to discover the mythical fruit of Mount Penglai, said to grant eternal life and even raise the dead. When he failed to find it, the emperor sent ships carrying hundreds of young people to try their luck. Legend has it that they stumbled upon Japan instead. Rather than return without an elixir and face the wrath of the emperor, they made Japan their new home. (Smart move.) Qin Shi Huang eventually died, likely from drinking—wait for it—longevity potions meant to make him immortal.

On to Plan B

Although he failed to find the secret to immortality here on Earth, Qin Shi Huang was prepared for his life after death. He'd been planning for it since he was 13 years old. In many ancient cultures, people were buried with items that might be useful in the afterlife. Qin Shi Huang went all out on his tomb so he'd be well protected from evil spirits. His burial spot was discovered in 1974, and archeologists have been excavating it ever since. The items they've turned up include 2,000 life-size clay soldiers, commonly called the Terracotta Warriors (experts believe there may be 8,000 in total). They've also found two large bronze chariots, 520 clay horses, and 40,000 bronze weapons.

LEGEND HAS IT

- In Egyptian mythology, gods consumed ambrosia, which allowed them to live forever. This food, said to be composed of honey and water, was brought to the gods each day by doves.

- The Moon rabbit is a prominent character in Chinese folklore. This creature spends its days creating an elixir of life for a Moon goddess named Chang'e.

- In Hindu mythology, a nectar called Amrita granted immortality. This elixir was found in the ocean. Gods and demons worked together to remove it from the waters.

- Idun, the goddess of spring in Norse mythology, was responsible for guarding sacred apples that the gods ate for eternal youth.

DO AWAY WITH DEATH

Most alchemists felt sure that if they worked hard enough in their laboratories, they could unlock the secrets of the natural world and, in doing so, discover an elixir to defeat death. They also placed some attention on finding a way to turn ordinary metals into gold. In their time, alchemists weren't given much respect. Many people perceived them as nothing more than sorcerers using black magic to stir up useless recipes. But these early scientists took their work seriously and were dedicated to their research.

Get In the Mix

In their efforts to create the elixir of life, alchemists made potions by mixing together ingredients like sulfur, arsenic, and liquid gold. But they put special focus on a substance called cinnabar. It seemed to have magical qualities, since it was bright red and transformed into a silvery liquid, called mercury, when heated. Although no alchemist produced an elixir of immortality, the work of these scientists was still useful. Their techniques and some of their tools are still used in chemistry labs today.

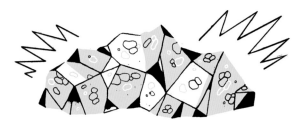

Meet an Alchemist... or Three

KO HUNG (283–343)

This Chinese alchemist and philosopher created a formula for eternal youth with cinnabar, which he believed was the ultimate ingredient for preventing illness and death. By ingesting it, he declared, "You will last as long as heaven and earth [and] be able to travel on clouds and ride dragons." Ko Hung died at age 60, which, although quite old for the time, was certainly not forever.

JÃBIR IBN HAYYÃN (721–815)

This Arabian alchemist popularized the term "elixir" (from the Arabic *al-iksir*, for "miracle substance"). In his immortality research, he focused on science and the importance of experimenting rather than on magic, unlike many others at the time. His work became well known in Europe, inspiring generations of future alchemists in their search for an elixir of life.

ROGER BACON (1214–1294)

This British scientist believed that short lifespans were caused by unhealthy lifestyles. According to Bacon, the easiest way to fix this was to avoid eating too much and to take healing medicines. He made these medicines from ingredients including gold, pearl, and coral. Bacon also suggested that people eat vipers, which were believed to have mystical powers.

Coming Soon to a Grocery Store Near You?

In 2010, the president of Kazakhstan called on scientists at a university in the country to find an elixir of life. After two years of study, they announced the creation of—drumroll, please—a yogurt-based drink called *nar*. Some experts suggest the drink might make people healthier and therefore help them live slightly longer. But yogurt is certainly not the elixir of eternal life the president was counting on.

FOREVER IN FICTION

The idea of extending life forever through an elixir also turns up in our novels and movies.

TUCK EVERLASTING
BY NATALIE BABBITT

In this 1975 novel, 10-year-old Winnie meets the Tucks, who have been granted eternal life after drinking from a spring beneath an old tree. But she comes to realize that living eternally isn't as perfect as it seems and decides not to live forever.

INDIANA JONES AND THE LAST CRUSADE

In this film from 1989, Indiana Jones searches for the Holy Grail, an ancient cup said to grant immortality to anyone who drinks from it. He finds the grail in a temple guarded by a 700-year-old knight. But for the cup to retain its power, it must stay within the temple.

A STONE'S THROW FROM FOREVER

While working on the elixir of immortality, many alchemists were also pursuing a mythical substance called the philosopher's stone. In fact, creating this stone was considered the magnum opus, or great work, for alchemists. It was their ultimate prize.

Can You Give Me Something to Go On?

Much mystery surrounds this substance. Even coming up with a description of the philosopher's stone is a challenge. Perhaps that's because there's no concrete proof that it even exists. (Just saying.) Some alchemists said it was a white stone, while others claimed it was blood red. And still others argued it wasn't a stone at all but a powder. The one thing alchemists agreed on was that the philosopher's stone had magical properties. It could transform a common metal, like lead, into a precious one, like gold or silver. And more importantly, it could be used to create the elixir of life.

Mission Accomplished?

A 14th-century French scholar named Nicolas Flamel is said to have created the philosopher's stone and, from there, the elixir of life. Flamel devoted 21 years to decoding a mysterious book of symbols. This book supposedly belonged to an Egyptian magician and contained secrets of alchemy. At the time, many believed Flamel had deciphered its contents to create the stone and achieve immortality for both himself and his wife. But Flamel's actions say otherwise. He designed his own tombstone while he was still alive, and it can be seen at his gravesite in Paris to this day. Even so, reports of Flamel sightings continued throughout the 17th and 18th centuries. And there are stories that his coffin was searched after his apparent death, only to find it was—gasp!—empty.

12

The great scientist Sir Isaac Newton (1642–1727) spent many hours studying Flamel's works. Newton's belief in the philosopher's stone recently came to light when historians stumbled upon a long-lost paper that described a recipe for making the stone.

Is There a Modern-Day Philosopher's Stone?

The fascination with the philosopher's stone didn't disappear after the Middle Ages. In 1975, an Arizona man named David Hudson found a white powdery material in soil on his property. After doing some research, Hudson suspected the substance might be the philosopher's stone. Eventually, a scientist from Cornell University analyzed it and found it was made up of iron, silica, and aluminum. Not exactly magical substances. But Hudson wasn't buying it. At a recent conference focused on modern alchemy, he explained that experts in Asia and Europe have refined the powder to create a medicine that has healing powers. On a side note, Hudson has never tried it himself.

THE STONE IS THE STAR

The intrigue of the philosopher's stone has led to its appearance in everything from novels and comics to video games and musical compositions. Perhaps the most well-known fictional reference to the stone is found in *Harry Potter and the Philosopher's Stone* (in the United States, *Harry Potter and the Sorcerer's Stone*). In this novel, the legendary substance plays a central role as Harry and his friends try to track it down. Interestingly, in the book, the stone is said to belong to a 665-year-old alchemist named Nicolas Flamel.

CLASS OF FOREVER

Meet an Immortal

If you dream of living forever, tracking down an immortal seems like a good idea. After all, he or she would certainly have the inside scoop on what it takes to make that happen.

There are many legends that center on immortals. And you'll come across characters in movies and literature who have managed to achieve extreme longevity. But what should we make of real-world stories about people who have apparently tacked decades or even centuries on to their lives? There's a tale of a British man who lived to be more than 150 years old, way back in the 16th century. And several individuals in the Old Testament were said to have lived well into their 900s. (Imagine the candles on those birthday cakes!) How seriously can we take these stories?

It's difficult to imagine people living to nearly 1,000 years old. And it's even harder to accept the idea of immortals among us. But many scientists are turning their attention to examples of immortality in our midst. They're currently studying creatures in the animal kingdom that never die, including a particular jellyfish and a microscopic organism called a hydra. If scientists can understand how it is that these animals live forever, perhaps they can use that information to help humans do the same. It's worth a try, some say.

When considering the possibility of immortality, it's probably worth getting to know some of those people, characters, and creatures who seem to have the whole living-forever thing—or at least, the living-an-awfully-long-time thing—figured out.

I CAN LIVE FOREVER. NOW WHAT?

You don't have to look too hard to find immortals in our myths and stories—from gods who battle atop a mountain to a blood-sucking nobleman in search of victims. But there's a surprising detail about some of these characters who have perfected the art of living forever: their immortal lives aren't perfect. In some cases, their stories show us that immortality doesn't guarantee a happily-ever-after.

Perhaps I Should Have Thought This Through

In Greek mythology, all gods were immortal. One myth, though, tells of a man's attempt at immortality. Tithonus, a human, falls in love with the goddess Eos. Eos asks Zeus, the king of the gods, to grant Tithonus eternal life so they can live together forever. Zeus grants her wish, but Eos failed to ask for Tithonus's eternal youth as well. Although Tithonus is immortal, his body continues to age. He becomes so frail that Eos can no longer watch him suffer and transforms him into a grasshopper… for eternity. Bummer.

Something Fishy about Forever

A young girl in the Japanese folktale called *Happyaku Bikuni* achieved immortality thanks to a fishlike creature known as a ningyo. It's described as a cross between an ugly, deformed human and a fish—similar to a mermaid, except it's repulsive to look at. The creature's flesh was said to bestow immortality on anyone who ate it. The girl ate ningyo meat, but throughout her long life, she had much sadness. She lived on while her husbands and children died. At the age of 800, she finally lost her will to live and passed away in spite of her immortality.

In the 1726 novel *Gulliver's Travels*, a group of immortals called the Struldbrugs do not die, but they do continue aging. Over time, they lose their memory, become weak, and lose friends. They envy those who can die.

Eight Is Great

According to Chinese folklore, a group known as the Eight Immortals lived on a cluster of islands near China. These people were born humans, but through intense meditation, they achieved immortality. The Eight Immortals included a scholar, a teenager, an elderly man, a woman, a poor man, an injured warrior, a philosopher, and a member of royalty. It's said they represented all members of Chinese society, proving anyone could achieve immortality.

IMMORTALS THROUGH THE PAGES

Meet these immortals found on the pages of books and comics.

DRACULA

This well-known vampire appears in a novel by Bram Stoker in 1897. He is capable of living forever, as long as he has a plentiful supply of victims and is not killed.

PETER PAN

First appearing in a 1904 play, this sometimes lonely boy lives on an enchanted island called Neverland, where he has unending youth.

ELVES AND WIZARDS OF MIDDLE-EARTH

Found in The Lord of the Rings, these immortal characters can die in battle, but they are capable of coming back from the dead. Author J.R.R. Tolkien said his book was about "the desire for deathlessness."

THE AMAZONS

In DC Comics, this is an all-female group of immortal warriors. The youngest of the Amazons, Princess Diana, gives up her immortality to fight evil. You know her better as Wonder Woman.

THE PAST AND FOREVER

It's hard to know where the truth begins and ends when it comes to stories about real people who have apparently lived extremely long lives. In most cases, the problem is that the individuals in question lived long ago, before birth and death records were common. Since their stories can't really be verified, this often makes tales of their long lives more mysterious than miraculous.

Now *That's* Old

In the Bible's Old Testament, there are many figures who lived centuries-long lives. Adam—of Adam and Eve fame—was supposed to have lived for 930 years. And the story goes that Noah—ark-builder extraordinaire—didn't sail off into his final sunset until he was 950. Then there's Methuselah, a man who is said to have reached the really ripe old age of 969.

Some people take the Bible literally and believe there was a time when humankind had extreme longevity. Others think these long lives are pure myth. And still others suggest that the ages of Adam, Noah, and Methuselah have been miscalculated over the years, and that, in the end, the men had an average lifespan for their time.

Stick to Your Veggies

During the 16th century, a man typically lived into his mid-30s. That's one of the reasons the story of Englishman Thomas Parr is so notable. It's claimed he lived for 152 years, from 1483 to 1635, thanks to a strict vegetarian diet. Old Parr or Old Tom Parr, as he was called, was a national celebrity because of his long life. He was even summoned to visit King Charles I in London. But after only a few weeks in the city, Parr passed away. A doctor at the time said that rich foods and the terrible pollution in London likely led to his death.

> Some believe that Parr was no older than 70, and that his recorded birthdate is actually that of his grandfather, who shared the same name.

An Immortal among Us?

A nobleman named Count of St-Germain became well known throughout the 1700s thanks to his claim that he owned the philosopher's stone. St-Germain traveled throughout Europe making "immortality potions" for the wealthy. Official records showed that he died in 1784 at the age of 74, yet many people claimed to have encounters with him after this date. Legends about his immortality became widespread in the late 19th and early 20th centuries. And as recently as 1972, someone came forward claiming to be St-Germain himself.

Words to Live…and Live…and Live By

Back in 1933, reports surfaced in *Time* magazine and the *New York Times* that a Chinese man named Li Ching-Yun had passed away after living 256 years. Of course, the extreme lifespan did raise some suspicions. It didn't help that Li himself said he had lived 197 years. But a professor at a Chinese university found records stating that Li was born in 1677, which would confirm the reported age. When asked before he died about his secret for living a long life, Li Ching-Yun said, "Keep a quiet heart, sit like a tortoise, walk sprightly like a pigeon, and sleep like a dog."

A French woman named Jeanne Calment lived to be 122 years old. Before she died in 1997, she said she owed her longevity in part to her good sense of humor.

ANIMALS KNOW BEST?

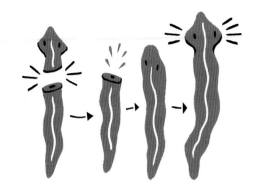

In an effort to unlock the key to living forever, scientists are focusing their research on animals that seem to have the inside track. Some members of the animal kingdom do not age. Researchers hope that by getting to the bottom of these species' immortality, they might just help humans live longer as well.

Naked Mole Rats

Although naked mole rats haven't got a lock on immortality, these rodents do live five times longer than other creatures their size. Researchers at the University of Rochester are studying the rats to determine the reason for their longevity. The belief is that their genes—as well as a thick chemical that surrounds and protects their cells—are the reason for their extra-long lives.

Planarian Worms

A biologist from England found that certain types of flatworms called planarians can constantly rebuild a section of their DNA (a molecule in cells that tells the body how to develop), and that this prevents them from aging. On top of this, they can even regrow their head, including their brain, if severed, and regain their original memories. Researchers determined this after noting that the worms remembered skills they had been trained to do—like crawl a specific route to get food—before being decapitated.

Turritopsis Dohrnii

The *Turritopsis dohrnii* species of jellyfish is only about the size of your pinky fingernail, but it knows a thing or two about immortality. It can transform from an adult to a baby over and over again. An expert who has studied *Turritopsis* once said it's like a butterfly that turns back into a caterpillar instead of dying. Researchers like Dr. Shin Kubota, a biologist at Kyoto University who has been studying this creature for nearly 20 years, are still trying to figure out this jellyfish's secret.

Scientists are looking closely at our genes for clues to immortality. A gene is a part of our cells that controls how the body grows and works. One gene that appears to play an important role in figuring out forever is the FoxO gene. It's involved in human aging, as well as in the longevity of other creatures.

In one study, scientists at a university in Germany determined that the FoxO gene is behind the immortality of the hydra, a microscopic sea animal. Found in fresh water from Europe to the Americas, this creature does not seem to die from old age. Scientists are now studying the hydra to better understand FoxO and learn the role it plays in aging.

Biologist Cynthia Kenyon from the University of California, San Francisco, is also focusing on this gene. She has managed to "turn off" the FoxO gene in microscopic worms called *C. elegans*. By doing this, Kenyon doubled their lifespan. (The worms typically live up to one month, but they survived for two in Kenyon's experiments.) Since humans also have the FoxO gene—or the fountain of youth gene, as it's sometimes referred to—Kenyon thinks she might be able to tweak it and extend our lives by decades.

In further studies from 2008 and 2009, researchers in both Honolulu and Germany found that people who live to 100 have a slight variation of a gene called FoxO3a. The findings suggest the gene may be strongly linked to a long life. Of course, it's likely that other genes and lifestyle factors also impact how long we live. And there is definite evidence that longevity runs in families. In a Boston University study of those who lived to 100 and beyond, researchers found that at least 50 percent had close relatives who also achieved very old age.

Genes are units inside our cells that tell our bodies how to develop.

Visit a Magical Place

Stories of legendary places that hold the key to immortality have been passed down through generations. And over time, many brave souls have set out in search of these sites, traveling far and wide for years upon end. They had no map, no guarantee—just the dream that they might discover a spot on this planet where it is possible to rid humankind of death.

As time has gone on and more of the globe is mapped, most of these fabled places have lost their mystique, and people now accept that they likely don't exist. But some spots, like the fountain of youth with its healing waters, still fascinate us and leave us wondering about the possibilities.

Today there are real-world places that have begun to stir up our curiosity. Longevity experts have found communities of people around the world who outlive most of us by decades. While these individuals haven't quite figured out how to live forever, they have certainly managed to live longer lives than the rest of us. Is there a way to unlock their secrets?

It's time to journey to some "magical" places—both legendary and real—that hold the promise of a long-lasting (or better yet, everlasting) life.

ON THE MAP

The search for places where immortality reigns has taken adventurers to all corners of the world. To this day, some of these destinations can be easily found on a map. But others were never proven to exist and remain the stuff of legends. These are a fcw of the places people sought in their pursuit of immortality.

A) BIMINI: Explorer Juan Ponce de León sailed throughout the Caribbean looking for Bimini, which was supposed to hold the fountain of youth. He landed in Florida by accident and never found Bimini or a magical spring. (Surprise.)

B) VENEZUELA: When Christopher Columbus landed in Venezuela in 1498, he was struck by the sheer size of its Orinoco River. In a letter to King Ferdinand and Queen Isabella of Spain, he wrote that he was certain it was a gateway to paradise on Earth.

C) ST. BRENDAN'S ISLAND: This mythical place intrigued many in the Middle Ages. It was said to be a place where the sun never set.

D) TÍR NA NÓG: Time was believed to stand still on this fabled island, and it's said that no one here ever grew old or suffered from any illness.

E) AVALON: This legendary island of immortals was first mentioned in the 1500s. Stories of its exact location changed throughout medieval times.

F) ABKHAZIA: Alexander the Great traveled through this so-called Land of Darkness in search of waters that made the old young again.

G) ETHIOPIA: Stories from 400 BCE tell of a group of people who were granted eternal life after bathing in a spring found here.

H) SOUTHERN TIP OF INDIA: In the Middle Ages, stories circulated about an earthly paradise that had a pool of eternal youth.

I) CHANG KONG CLIFF ROAD: This narrow pathway was built on the face of a cliff so people could search for a society of immortals believed to be living deep in the mountains of China.

DRINK UP TO LIVE ON

You've likely heard the fable of the fountain of youth—said to restore youth to anyone who drinks or bathes in its waters. (Talk about refreshing!) Rumors of this magical pool and its healing powers have persisted for centuries. Although no one has ever found the wellspring, it intrigues us to this day. Perhaps we're captivated by the mystery of a secret place, hidden like a buried treasure waiting to be discovered.

The Fountain through the Ages

The fountain of youth can be traced back to at least 700 BCE. A Hindu legend from that time tells the story of a priest named Cyavanna. He entered into a "pool of youth" and was instantly transformed into a young man. And Greek historian Herodotus (5th century BCE) recounted the tale of legendary tribespeople in Ethiopia who lived long lives thanks to bathing in a violet-scented spring.

My Empire for a Fountain of Youth!

Alexander the Great, the ruler of a Greek kingdom who conquered much of the world before he died around 323 BCE, was said to have gone on his own quest to find the "water of life." In one version of the legend, Alexander sets off on an expedition and comes upon four men who tell him about a pool that restores youth. Alexander finds it and takes a dip. And as promised, he becomes a young man again.

You've Got Mail

The hunt for the fountain of youth intensified in 1165 when a letter was sent to prominent people of the time, including the pope, several emperors, and a number of European monarchs. It came from a man named Prester John, who claimed to rule a lost nation somewhere in India. The mysterious letter explained that Prester John's kingdom was paradise on Earth, and home to a river of gold and a pool whose waters provided "lasting health and the renewal of youth." It sparked centuries of exploration across Asia and Africa, but no one ever found it—or Prester John.

> In the Pirates of the Caribbean film series, Jack Sparrow gets caught up in the myth and embarks on a quest to find the fountain of youth.

Find the Fountain

The person most associated with the fountain of youth is Spanish explorer Juan Ponce de León. The story goes that he heard about an island known as Bimini (see page 24), where a spring gushed with magical water. Ponce de León sailed among the islands of the Bahamas, only to accidentally land in Florida in 1513. He then returned to Spain. In 1521, he set off on another expedition, but was fatally wounded in a battle. Despite being the person most closely linked to the fountain, Ponce de León was most likely never focused on finding the spring. Instead, many historians suggest he was looking to secure land and gold.

STEP RIGHT UP— GET YOUR MAGICAL WATER HERE!

Today, the city of St. Augustine, Florida—the site where Ponce de León first landed—has a tourist attraction dedicated to the fountain of youth and the Spanish explorer himself. Ponce de León's Fountain of Youth Archaeological Park even features a spring that visitors can drink from. For those who'd rather get it to go, a gift shop sells bottles of the spring's "magical" water.

MODERN-DAY MIRACLES?

The days of sailing away to discover a pool that bestows everlasting life may be a thing of the past, but we haven't quite given up on finding a place that will help us live forever, or at least longer. Researchers have turned their attention to regions around the world where people tend to live longer and healthier lives than most—so-called Blue Zones.

Exploring the Blue Zones

The concept of Blue Zones came about in the mid 2000s thanks to an American researcher and modern-day explorer named Dan Buettner. He'd traveled the world and was intrigued by the fact that people in five specific places have a greater life expectancy than those living anywhere else, with many reaching the age of 100. Buettner teamed with longevity experts and scientists to find out why.

He discovered that people in Blue Zones share similar life habits. They get daily exercise simply by walking and gardening regularly. They eat a healthy, modest diet. And they focus on socializing with family and friends, having a spiritual life, taking time to rest, and pursuing goals that make them happy.

Blue Zones at a Glance

SARDINIA, ITALY:
- This island is home to the world's longest-living men—many reach age 100.
- People often walk up to 5 miles (8 km) per day on rugged terrain.
- Their diet consists mainly of goat's milk and cheese, fava beans, and barley.

OKINAWA, JAPAN:
- This group of islands was once known as a land of immortals.
- A common saying before every meal is *Hara hachi bu*. This means "Eat until you are 80 percent full."

NICOYA PENINSULA, COSTA RICA:
- This is the biggest Blue Zone in the world.
- It's home to hundreds of centenarians (people who live to the age of 100 or beyond)—more than anywhere else on Earth.

IKARIA, GREECE:
- This small, isolated island has the highest percentage of 90-year-olds on Earth.
- Afternoon naps are common here.

LOMA LINDA, CALIFORNIA:
- In this small town, people live longer than those anywhere else in the United States.
- Residents are predominantly vegetarian.
- There is an emphasis on volunteering to encourage positivity.

THE DIRT ON AGING

Scientists have found that Easter Island, in the southeastern Pacific Ocean, may be home to a "soil of youth." A natural bacteria called rapamycin is found in the island's soil. After this bacteria's discovery in 1966, researchers learned it could be used medically, helping prevent organ rejection in transplant patients. And in 2011, a study showed that rapamycin extends the lifespan of lab mice by up to 38 percent. Some researchers believe this bacteria, if turned into an anti-aging pill, could extend human life by a decade.

Centenarians are one of the fastest-growing groups of people in our society. It's estimated that by 2030, there will be one million people on the planet pushing 100 years old. According to several studies, four out of five centenarians are women.

Hang In There

There's a popular saying: "Patience is a virtue." Basically, this means that being patient is a good thing. You'll definitely need it if you're waiting for an answer for how to live forever. Although scientists are working away on immortality research, there's no magic formula for eternal life in sight.

Of course, as we wait, we are continuing to age. At this point, if we are truly interested in living forever, it's probably best to stop focusing on the forever part. Instead, we may do better to think about just the next few decades. If we can extend our lives a bit, maybe, just maybe, we'll be on the planet when an immortality breakthrough does come along.

In the meantime, how do we go about adding those few decades to our lives?

A number of experts are intent on halting the aging process. They're trying to fine-tune the human body to boost our health and, in turn, our longevity.

And then there's the ultimate "wait it out" approach to immortality. Some people have arranged for their bodies to be frozen after their death. They figure they will chill out until science is so advanced that doctors can bring them back to life and cure all that ails them.

This chapter looks at some of the ways we might increase our lifespan—so we'll be around if anyone discovers the trick to living forever.

AN AGE-OLD QUESTION

Scientists and their anti-aging studies may be one of the best hopes for lengthening our lives. There are many whose main goal is to stop aging altogether, whether by changing the way our bodies work or by discovering a pill that will help us achieve this. Wishful thinking? For many experts, it's a question not of *if* we can stop aging but of *when* wc will figure out how to do it.

Built to Age

American biologist William Andrews has spent much of his career searching for a way to stop aging. He has paid particular attention to a segment of DNA called telomeres (pronounced *TEE-low-meers*). Telomeres are found on the ends of our chromosomes (threadlike structures that carry our genes). They protect our genes and keep chromosome ends from fraying—some people liken them to the plastic sheaths that keep the ends of shoelaces from unraveling. As we age, our telomeres shorten. When they get too short, our cells wear out and can no longer divide. That leads to the weakening of our tissues and organ systems, and it's why we become more vulnerable to aging and disease.

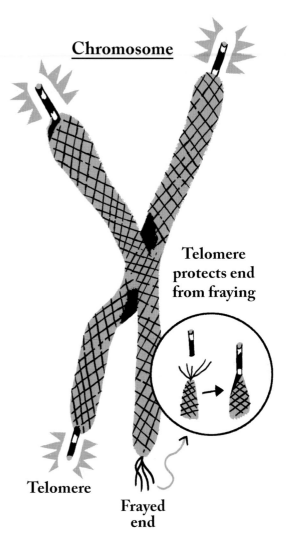

Chromosome

Telomere protects end from fraying

Telomere

Frayed end

Dr. Andrews led a team of researchers in identifying a gene called telomerase (pronounced *tull-OM-uh-rays*). It produces a protein that lengthens telomeres as soon as they are shortened, preventing cells from wearing out. Only certain cells produce the telomerase protein. But here's where it gets really interesting. The researchers also discovered that all our cells have the *ability* to produce it. Now Dr. Andrews is on a mission to find a chemical or drug to "switch on" the telomerase gene in *all* our cells. If this is successful, it may help reverse aging and increase the human lifespan by decades or more.

Let Them Eat Grapes

In 2008, researchers began studying a substance called resveratrol in hopes of helping us live longer lives. Resveratrol is found in certain foods, like red grapes, berries, peanuts, and cocoa. A recent study at Harvard Medical School showed that it helps our bodies produce a protein called SIRT1, which is said to improve how our cells function. So far, researchers have used resveratrol in studies with lab rats, successfully extending their lifespans. Other studies couldn't duplicate those results, though, so a resveratrol anti-aging pill is still far from reality.

Dracula Would Approve

Longevity scientists at Stanford University are testing young blood therapy—also known as vampire therapy. In this treatment, blood from young lab mice is placed in older mice to see if this reverses the signs of aging. Early results seem to show that the young blood "recharges" the brains of the aging mice.

MAKE THE SWITCH

At King's College London, researchers have discovered four "Father Time" genes that control how fast we age. These aging genes are switched on or off by factors in our daily life, such as diet and the environment around us. The trick now is for researchers to see if they can find a way to control these genes, which could potentially stop the aging process entirely.

It's in the Blood

Scientists at Harvard University have had some promising results in their studies with a molecule known as GDF11. This protein is found in our bloodstream, and it keeps our brain and muscles young and strong. We have a lot of GDF11 in our blood when we are young, but the amount decreases as we age. In lab studies, Harvard researchers increased the levels of the protein in older mice. This helped restore aging muscles and improved the performance of the brain. Scientists are looking to begin human studies with GDF11 as early as 2017. It's hoped there will be similar anti-aging results in humans.

ON THE PATH TO ETERNITY

While we wait for a groundbreaking discovery that'll get us a step closer to living forever, there are things we can start doing now to have a shot at a longer life. The foods we eat and the choices we make in our daily lives can both impact our longevity. Sometimes small changes can be our ticket to adding a few extra years to our lifetime.

Some studies have shown that healthy eating habits can slow cell aging, giving people a better chance at a longer life.

Food for Thought

There's evidence to suggest that what we put on our plate can play a role in extending our lifespan. Some foods are better than others at warding off disease and helping us with our overall health and longevity.

BLUEBERRIES are packed with natural substances called flavonoids, which protect our memory and keep us heart-healthy. In a 1999 study at Tufts University in Massachusetts, researchers fed blueberries to rats to see if this impacted their aging. They found that the rats had better balance and coordination when they reached old age than rats that didn't eat the fruit.

WILD SALMON contains omega-3s, a healthy kind of fat that helps with brain development, bone health, and blood circulation. This fish is a main staple in the diet of the Yup'ik people in Alaska. A recent study suggests that diet is the main reason the Yup'ik rarely face illnesses such as diabetes and heart disease.

DARK CHOCOLATE can work wonders, since it improves blood flow and lowers the risk of heart disease. The Kuna people, who live on islands off the coast of Panama, have a much lower rate of heart disease than those who live on the mainland. It's believed this is because the Kuna drink more than five cups of natural cocoa a day. They make the chocolate powder for their drink from raw cacao beans they grow themselves.

WATERMELON is high in a nutrient called lycopene (pronounced *LIE-cah-peen*). It's said to help fight cancer and heart disease. According to experts, we'll get more benefit from watermelon if we store it out of the fridge. That's because watermelon produces more lycopene at room temperature than when it is chilled.

Live It Up

What you eat may help grant you a longer life, but there are other simple choices that can also put you on that path. From finding a fluffy friend to caring for your pearly whites, experts have found there are things entirely under your control that can give you added time on the planet.

MAKE A RUN FOR IT: Regular exercise keeps your body fit, helps your immune system fight off infections, and can fend off a number of health problems. A study published in 2014 found that running just five to ten minutes a day can increase an individual's lifespan.

GET A PET: Research suggests that owning a pet leads to a longer life. A recent study of cat owners found they have fewer heart attacks and less heart disease. And owning a dog can also lower your risk of health troubles. Pets help reduce our stress, and less stress generally means a healthier you.

DENTIST KNOWS BEST: Experts say that flossing your teeth regularly can add up to six years to your life. Flossing keeps harmful bacteria from being released into the bloodstream and affecting your health.

CATCH SOME ZZZZs: Some experts have found that adults can increase their lifespan by getting six or seven hours of sleep each night. And a 2002 study at the University of California, San Diego, reported that adults who frequently get less than seven hours of sleep per night have a higher risk of developing illnesses like diabetes or heart disease.

C'MON, GET HAPPY: In 2012, a study at a university in New York determined that certain personality traits play a part in longevity—especially being friendly, optimistic, easygoing, and quick to laugh.

GIVING DEATH THE COLD SHOULDER

In the 1960s, an American man named Robert Ettinger wrote about the concept of freezing the human body after death so that it could be brought back to life in the future. The practice, called cryonics, is based on the theory that medicine will one day become so advanced that a doctor will be able to revive a preserved body and restore it to good health. Immortality at last!

Ettinger's work received a lot of publicity in the late 1960s. When people began to look closely at the science behind his concept, some became convinced that it was worth a try. In 1967, a doctor named James Bedford became the first person to be cryogenically frozen. Cryonics companies began to spring up in the late 1970s, including one formed by Ettinger himself. In 1977, his mom became its first frozen patient.

Into the Deep Freeze

Today, over 200 people have been cryogenically frozen, including Robert Ettinger, who died in 2011. Of course, you can't just toss a person into a freezer and be done with it. Creating human icicles is a careful and scientific process. To properly preserve a body, a team at a cryonics facility first removes the water from the blood vessels, replacing it with a chemical that will protect cells, organs, and tissues in extremely low temperatures. From there, the body is cooled on a bed of dry ice. Finally, it's placed inside a large metal tank filled with liquid nitrogen that's a frosty -211°F (-135°C). It should be noted that, as of yet, no one has been revived from this frozen state.

The most famous person to be frozen after death is baseball legend Ted Williams. It's commonly believed that Walt Disney was also cryogenically frozen, though this is not true.

If You Build It, They Will Freeze

An American man named Saul Kent has been intrigued by cryonics since he first heard Robert Ettinger discussing it on a radio show in the 1960s. Now he plans to build the world's largest facility dedicated to cryonics. Named the Timeship, the building is expected to cover 6 acres (2.5 ha). The plan is for it to house up to 10,000 cryogenically frozen people, as well as cryopreserved animal and plant DNA. The structure will also be home to research laboratories, where experts will dedicate their studies to life extension and, ultimately, finding the key to human immortality. Set to open in Texas, the Timeship project is still in its design stage.

THE BIG CHILL

The idea of freezing and then reviving people seems a bit like something out of the movies. But you might be surprised to learn that cooling therapies are in use in hospitals. A treatment known as therapeutic hypothermia helps people who have gone into cardiac arrest—that's when a heart suddenly and unexpectedly stops beating. Once the heart rhythm has been restored, special cooling devices are used to lower the patient's body temperature and put him or her in a state that is somewhat like hibernation. This therapy protects the brain from damage that can occur after cardiac arrest because of a lack of blood flow. Generally, after 24 hours, the patient is slowly rewarmed to a normal body temperature and, if all goes well, soon returns to consciousness.

Look to the Future

Be warned—these ideas are pretty out there. But if we're going to examine all the possible ways to live forever, we have to cover every angle.

Since we haven't had much luck with achieving immortality in the past few thousand years, some people are looking to the future. Many are considering technological immortality—that is, finding a way to merge technology with the body to create a superhuman who will never die.

Some people have tossed around the idea of transferring the contents of the brain to a robot to make a digitally immortal "human." Another thought is to use technology to produce a new kind of human body, one that has eternal life. There's even a scientist who has already created, within a computer, a digital copy of himself that will exist long after he dies.

Many other people, however, believe that there's a future in store for us beyond what we make with machines. This is spiritual immortality. At the heart of many religions is the notion of an afterlife in which your soul or spirit—rather than your body—lives forever. Think of it as a form of everlasting life that's not of this planet.

Let's open our minds a bit and see where the search for immortality takes us.

BEYOND THE BODY

Some people will do whatever it takes to achieve immortality, including bypassing the body altogether. They are prepared to focus on the mind and find a way to keep it alive when the body fails. After all, our mind is a big part of who we are—holding our memories, our thoughts, and our sense of self. So if we are serious about living forever, perhaps the mind is where it's at.

A New Human

A Russian billionaire recently created an organization that's focused on achieving immortality within the next 30 years. Called the 2045 Initiative, one of its main projects is mind uploading. This involves copying the contents of a person's brain onto a computer chip and placing it in an avatar, or a human-like robot. Mind uploading would create a digital version of a human being that could live forever. Eventually, the organization hopes to go even further, creating hologram-like bodies that contain a digital human brain. This would allow one holographic body to transfer its mind to another holographic body somewhere else in the world just by thinking about it. More superhero than human, this new "species" would be able to walk through walls and move at the speed of light.

Forever...or Not?

Although mind uploading seems a little—okay, a lot—like science fiction, many think it's simply an innovative way to make humans immune to death. But others raise questions about a possible human-robot combo. What would this mean for the human race? What if several individuals' brains were put on the same computer chip and then placed inside an avatar? Could this lead to the merging of two or more people into one "person"? And what about the possibility of a virus completely wiping out an individual in the same way a virus corrupts a computer's hard drive? That would end "forever" really quickly.

Uploading a human brain to a robot may be decades away, but some experts are already ahead of the game. Engineers from the Universities of Sheffield and Sussex in England are preparing to scan the brains of bees and upload them into robots that will (hopefully) fly and act like the real thing.

The Next Best Thing to Being There?

Jason Leigh, a computer scientist at the University of Illinois, is leading a team of researchers in creating digital versions of people, or avatars, that will exist on a computer. The goal of Project LifeLike is to create avatars that communicate as if they are living, breathing people. For this, Leigh makes a 3-D version of a person, capturing the appearance, voice, facial expressions, and body language. Plus, each avatar is programmed with a person's thoughts, feelings, and memories. This virtual, or computer-generated, replica preserves the mind of a person rather than the body. If all goes as planned, the virtual person will be capable of having conversations with future generations long after the real person has passed on.

Hey! That's Me! (Sort of…)

Jason Leigh has already successfully made a virtual avatar of himself that "lives" inside a computer. This replica has Leigh's mannerisms, memories, knowledge, and sense of humor. And it can speak and answer questions. There's no denying that the avatar is an amazing accomplishment. But it will never be fully human in the way that we are human. It doesn't have emotions. It can communicate only based on how it has been programmed. And it can't evolve or create new memories. Still, how remarkable would it be to talk to "yourself," and to know that others may be able to chat with "you" in the future?

A BETTER BODY

One of the best-known authorities on immortality is computer scientist and inventor Ray Kurzweil. He is a futurist—a person who studies the future and makes predictions about it. Kurzweil believes humans will be immortal by 2030. He focuses on a theory called singularity, which is the moment when humans will merge with computers. He and others talk about creating a body that is part technological and part human. They suggest that this modified body will be so resilient it will not die.

Built to Last

We have already been improving upon the human body for years. Today, artificial arms and legs are common, as are knee and hip replacements. Scientists have created robotic limbs that move like the real thing, and medical tests have begun on a specialized "eye" that can restore vision to the blind. But whether we can change the human body so drastically that we become immortal remains to be seen.

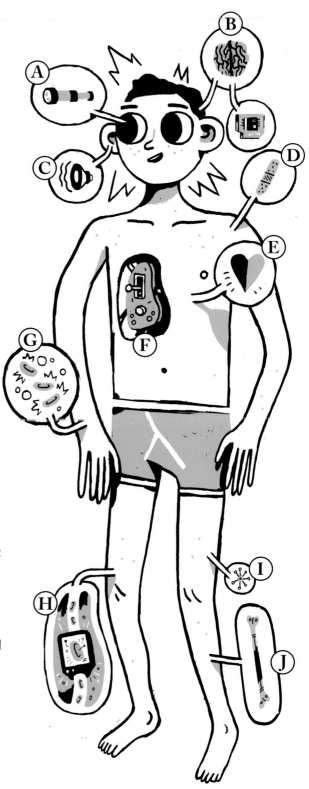

The Human Body of the Future?

Here's how technology could be used in the future to make humans immortal.

A) EYES: Monitors added to our eyes could improve our vision.

B) BRAIN: Computer chips and processors implanted in the brain could help us recall data easily, download information, and communicate with others through thought.

C) EARS: Implants in our ears would give us superior hearing.

D) SKIN: Smart skin might heal almost instantly and include sun protection.

E) HEART: The heart might be removed completely, and blood cell-sized robots called nanorobots would be put in charge of blood flow.

F) LUNGS: Nanorobots would replace the lungs, providing oxygen to and removing carbon dioxide from the blood.

G) BLOOD CELLS: Artificial blood cells would carry more oxygen and carbon dioxide, allowing us to hold our breath under water for hours and run at top speed without getting winded.

H) BLOODSTREAM: Sensors added to our bloodstream might monitor the specific nutrients we need.

I) THE ENTIRE BODY: Futurists predict nanorobots will be coursing through our bodies by the 2020s. They'll keep us in perfect health by supplying nourishment and caring for our cells and organs.

J) SKELETON: Bones would be self-repairing and stronger with help from nanorobots.

Make a Copy

Cloning is a process that allows scientists to make genetic copies of an organism. The technique involves taking cells from two creatures, fusing them together, and placing the new cell inside another creature to develop. No one has cloned a human yet, but we have been successful in creating frogs, mice, and sheep.

There are two approaches to cloning. The first focuses on cloning new, healthy organs or tissues. That way, if a body part fails, it can be replaced in the same way you might replace a part on a car. The second approach is cloning a full-grown body. This would allow for the brain of an older person to be placed inside a younger body, so he or she could live a longer life. There is much controversy surrounding cloning because some people believe it treats living creatures like objects.

NEXT STOP: THE AFTERLIFE

Spending eternity on Earth is something most of us can't quite wrap our minds around. But what about an eternal life after death? This form of immortality is at the core of most of the world's major religions. There are those who suggest that humans came up with the idea of an afterlife because the thought of dying is too frightening. That said, billions of people have faith that they will live on in another form after they die. Here's what a few religions say about spiritual immortality.

Hinduism

According to the Hindu religion, people repeat a cycle of birth, life, death, and rebirth. The ultimate goal is to end this cycle and free the soul so it can reach eternal oneness with the spirit of the creator god, Brahma. This is said to be achieved by living a life of perfection—one focused entirely on goodness and spirituality.

Christianity

The majority of Christians believe that after death, a person's soul is raised to heaven, a peaceful place where there is no sadness. Eternity is spent here in the presence of God. There is also said to be an eternal home for those who have lived a sinful, or evil, life—known as hell.

Islam

Muslims, those who follow Islam, believe that after death, the soul will be admitted into Jannah—a paradise where everyone is promised immortality. Those who have led a life of sin will enter into a hell-like place called Jahannam, but they may be released to paradise at some point if God sees fit.

A recent study at Boston University found that our belief in an eternal afterlife is actually a natural human instinct, not learned through religion, school, or media.

Buddhism

Buddhism teaches that there is an ongoing cycle of birth, life, death, and rebirth. That means the essence of a person comes back again and again within another body. The only way to break out of this cycle is to achieve enlightenment—a state of nothingness, or perfect peace. This is not a place, like heaven. It is really about becoming one with the universe itself.

Judaism

The Jewish afterlife is called olam ha-ba, which means "the world to come." But since Judaism focuses on earthly life, Jewish sacred books don't say much about the afterlife. Some Jews believe worthy souls go to a place similar to a Christian heaven. Others think that wicked souls are destroyed at death. And there are those who believe that people are reborn over many lifetimes.

BE PREPARED

Cultures around the world have numerous rituals when it comes to their dead and an eternal afterlife.

VIETNAM: Fake money is placed under rocks near buried relatives so that they can buy what they need in their next life.

CAMBODIA AND THAILAND: Food and drinks are left in front of homes, in case the souls of dead family members get hungry.

BRITAIN, IRELAND, AND CENTRAL EUROPE: In centuries past, tribes from these areas left windows and doors wide open when a person died. This was done to provide a clear path for the soul as it traveled to the next world.

NORTH AMERICA: At one time, some Aboriginal tribes buried their dead in the fetal position—like a baby in the womb—to prepare the body for its rebirth into the afterlife.

ANCIENT EGYPT: Bodies were preserved through mummification—wrapping them as mummies. This ensured that the dead could use their bodies in the afterlife. Egyptians also buried their dead with items they might need in eternal life, such as food, weapons, and tools.

CONCLUSION
The Last Word on Forever

You may wonder if we're any closer to answering the question, How can we live forever? After examining everything from potions and immortals to genes and future technology, the answer is a resounding… um, not really.

The plain and simple truth is that although human beings have dedicated themselves to the quest for immortality for centuries, we have not managed to make everlasting life a reality. At least, not yet.

There are some who say we will never find a way to live forever. Take American biologist Leonard Hayflick, for instance. He conducted an experiment in the 1960s and found that normal human cells divide a certain number of times. Then cell division stops completely. His theory, known as the Hayflick limit, holds that humans are biologically made to have a limited lifespan. So no matter what we do, forever is impossible.

On the other side are those who suggest that human beings have achieved many things once believed to be impossible.

Futurist Ray Kurzweil reminds us that predictions he made in the 1990s—like the invention of self-driving cars and phones that answer your questions—were scoffed at by many people at the time. In the end, he was right. So he and others suggest that it's entirely possible for humans to make a discovery that will allow us to cheat death.

With all that being said, we should consider the issues that might come up if we ever manage to achieve immortality. What would life be like for us? Would we get bored living year after year after (yawn…) year? Would we become too overwhelmed with the never-ending stresses and responsibilities of life once we hit, say, 1,000 years old? And exactly where would we put everybody? If everyone lived forever, the Earth would become awfully cramped. Would we have to colonize underground or in outer space?

Finally, while we're asking how to live forever, we should also ask why we want to live forever. What makes human beings so desperate to defy death?

It could be something as simple as a fear of dying. Or maybe it's the fact that humans are natural-born problem solvers and see death as something we must fix. Perhaps it's just that we're a curious bunch who want to experience endless possibilities and opportunities.

Whatever the reason, the human race refuses to take no—or death—for an answer. If nothing else, you've got to give us credit. We have an unshakeable belief in ourselves and our abilities. Can we really learn how to outdo death and live forever?

The only way to know is to stick around and find out.

INDEX

Acknowledgments

A sincere thanks to everyone at Owlkids Books, especially Karen Li for your help in shaping this book at the outset, Jessica Burgess for your guidance and attention to detail, and Alisa Baldwin for the engaging design. Thank you to John Crossingham for your valuable direction as I wrote my way through these pages. Much appreciation to Josh Holinaty for your brilliant artwork, and to Dana Murchison for your helpful comments. And many thanks to the Ontario Arts Council for your generous support of this project through the Writers' Reserve. While I used many resources in my research, two books were extremely enlightening—Adam Gollner's The Book of Immortality and The Quest for Immortality by S. Jay Olshansky and Bruce A. Carnes. With thanks to the authors for their insight. And, as always, thank you to Sam and Grace—you are my forever.